First published 2017
by Bloomsbury Publishing Plc
50 Bedford Square, London WC1B 3DP
www.bloomsbury.com

ISBN 978-1-4088-8747-9

A CIP catalogue for this book is available from the British Library.

Printed in China by Leo Paper Products, Heshan, Guangdong

1 3 5 7 9 10 8 6 4 2

TWEET QUACK MOO

Fatima Sharafeddine

Illustrated by Hassan Zahreddine

BLOOMSBURY
CHILDREN'S
BOOKS

1

One little bird tweeting on a treetop
Tweet...

2

Two ducks swimming in a pond

Quack...Quack...

3

Three chickens pecking at some grains
Cluck...Cluck...Cluck

Four cats looking for milk

Meow...Meow...Meow...Meow

5

Five rabbits munching carrots
Crunch...Crunch...Crunch...
Crunch...Crunch

6

Six dogs playing in the field
Woof...Woof...Woof...Woof...
Woof...Woof

Seven sheep bleating in the meadow
Baa...Baa...Baa...Baa...
Baa...Baa...Baa

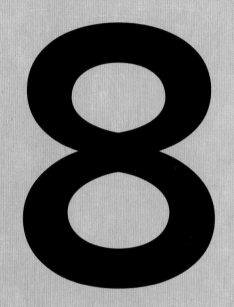

Eight monkeys picking bananas

Ooh...Ooh...Ooh... Ooh...Ooh...Ooh... Ooh...Ooh

9

Nine horses race

Neigh... Neigh... Neigh... Neigh... Neigh...
Neigh... Neigh... Neigh... Neigh...

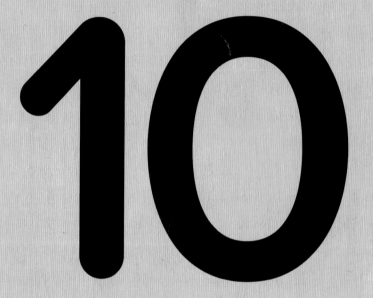

10

Ten cows sunbathing on the grass

Moo... Moo... Moo... Moo... Moo...
Moo... Moo... Moo... Moo... Moo...